NORMAN D. STOLPE

in the company of

ANGELS

WHAT THE BIBLE TEACHES
WHAT YOU NEED TO KNOW

LEADER'S GUIDE

CRC Publications
Grand Rapids, Michigan

ACKNOWLEDGMENTS

We are grateful to Norman D. Stolpe, minister of Christian education at the First Presbyterian Church of Mt. Holly, New Jersey, for writing this leader's guide.

We also thank Andrew Bandstra for writing the student book for this course. Bandstra is Professor of New Testament, Emeritus, Calvin Theological Seminary, Grand Rapids, Michigan.

CONTENTS

LEADING THIS COURSE

Angels, it seems, have winged their way into just about everyone's heart these days. According to a recent *Time* magazine poll, 6 percent of Americans believe that angels exist and 46 percent believe they have their own personal guardian angel. Some bookstores devote whole sections to books about angels. Angels appear in movies, are discussed on talk shows, and adorn the shelves of gift shops. Just about everyone has heard an angel story or two. And not a few of us are convinced we've personally been in the company of angels.

All this enthusiasm about angels will probably net you a large group of interested adults for your class. Some may come because they're fascinated with the mystery and intrigue of angels. They may have experienced the presence of an angel in their own lives. Others may be skeptical, feeling that—in the words of Martin Marty—"It was easier to believe in angels before they started popping up all over" (*Context*, November 13, 1994). Still others may want to find out for themselves exactly what the Bible says about angels.

This course will certainly include stories of angel visits. But, like the textbook on which it is based, it will avoid speculation about the nature of angels. And it will stick closely to what the Bible teaches and what we need to know.

GOALS OF THIS COURSE

This thirteen-session course should help participants

- develop biblically accurate expectations for the work of angels in the world and in the lives of people

- use the Bible to evaluate popular ideas and stories about angels

- be more aware of and awed by the power of God in our world

- gain strength for their own spiritual struggles

USING THE TEXT

All group members should have a copy of *In the Company of Angels* by Andrew Bandstra. You'll want to encourage everyone to read the chapters of this book at home each week. The sessions are not built on a detailed discussion of the text; instead this guide provides a range of activities that are meaningful on their own. However, reading the text prior to class will greatly enhance and deepen your discussions together.

INTRODUCTORY SESSION

We suggest distributing the text at the conclusion of the introductory session (session 1). In addition to introducing the text, this special session will help motivate people for the course, identify their concerns and questions about angels, and understand the purpose of this study.

Please see session 1 of this guide for details.

LEADER'S ROLE

This course emphasizes group participation and discussion. A typical session will be less like a formal, structured "class" and more like a group of adults meeting together for discussion. You and the others will be working together.

You should have at least forty-five minutes for each session, though an hour is preferable. Please adapt these materials to fit your time schedule and the interests of the adults in your group. We fully expect that you'll be ignoring some of our suggestions and substituting your own approaches from time to time. In short, use this guide as more of a resource than a recipe.

Each session begins with **Session Goals.** Look at these as you plan which activities to include in your session. You may want to look again after the session to determine how many of the goals you were able to meet.

The **Materials** section lists all the items you'll need to lead the session. These include *In the Company of Angels*, Bibles, newsprint pad, markers, and other items. You may also want to have a "hospitality table" with refreshments for people to enjoy as they arrive.

To help people feel welcome right from the start, you may want to offer an **Arrival Activity** just prior to each session. These optional activities are described in detail in each session. They give people something worthwhile and engaging to do as soon as they arrive. They end with a time of sharing concerns and praying for each other.

Each session begins with an **Imaginative Exploration.** It may involve sharing of experiences or stories about angels; it may call for a group response to a key question or quotation; it may solicit a reaction to a comment in the text. From time to time, you may want to use the arrival activity in place of the imaginative exploration activity. If you do that, make sure the exploration activity isn't essential to the steps that follow it.

The **Reality Check** is the heart of the session. It consists of examining the biblical evidence on a given issue or topic. Often the passages have been discussed by Andrew Bandstra in the text, which can be used for reference during your discussion.

The session ends with **Personal Connection.** Participants focus on how this particular discussion about angels affects our beliefs, our attitudes, our actions. A key part of this time is keeping track of a list of questions about angels developed by participants at the beginning of the course that they would like to see answered. The questions are "checked off" as the group discusses them throughout the course. Suggestions are given for closing each session with prayer. Participants are then asked to read the chapter in *In the Company of Angels* to be discussed next time.

SUBGROUPS

You will find numerous suggestions for working in subgroups of two to five persons each. This is done (a) to involve all the participants to a greater degree, (b) to help people get to know and care about each other, and (c) to make your job easier. You'll find that working in subgroups is especially important if you have, say, fifteen or twenty or more persons attending.

Small group work will go better if you follow a few simple suggestions:

- Vary the makeup of the groups from session to session.

- Take the time to explain exactly what you want the groups to do.

- If groups are to answer questions, display a list of these questions on newsprint.

- When appropriate, have each group appoint someone to jot down its key findings on newsprint.

- Give a definite time limit for groups to finish. Proceed with the next part of the session, even though all groups may not be finished.

- Be available to answer questions, clarify instructions, and so on while the small groups meet.

Use small groups as you and the others find them useful and comfortable.

EVALUATION

As leader, you would do well to ask the group from time to time, "How are we doing?" Give people a chance to react to your use of group time and to the book. Is there anything they would like to do differently? Is there a process they would like repeated because they found it particularly meaningful or effective? Be candid and open with the group as you discuss how the sessions might be improved.

We would also be interesting in hearing how your group is doing. We invite you to send your reactions, suggestions, or questions to

CRC Publications
2850 Kalamazoo Ave. SE
Grand Rapids, MI 49560

INTRODUCTION

SESSION GOALS

- to help participants make a personal connection to the study of angels from a biblical perspective

- to motivate people to pursue this study of *In the Company of Angels* by participating in group activities and by looking at the relevant biblical material

- to identify questions about angels for which participants would like to find answers during this course

MATERIALS

- Collection of "angels" from art, craft, and commercial sources

- Bibles for all participants (encourage them to bring their own)

- Hospitality table supplies

- Newsprint pad

- Markers

- Masking tape

- Copies of *In the Company of Angels* by Andrew Bandstra (one per person or couple)

Note: This is an introductory session. You will be giving participants a copy of In the Company of Angels at the end of the session.

ARRIVAL ACTIVITY

People often feel a little unsure of what to expect when they begin a new program. They may wonder whether this course will be valuable or interesting. They may be concerned about who else will be there and what the leader will be like. The first several minutes can be particularly awkward as participants wait for others to come, perhaps wondering if they have found the right meeting place.

As group leader, you can do a lot to relieve these anxieties and get this course off to an energetic start. To help people feel confident that they are in the right place, arrive early and have your materials organized. A sign identifying the course and yourself as leader will help people be comfortable from the moment they walk in the room.

Another way to make people feel welcome right from the beginning is to set up a hospitality table: coffee, hot water, tea bags, chocolate mix, spoons, cups, napkins, fruit pieces, cookies, bagels.

A well-organized, interesting activity to involve people the minute they arrive is one the best ways to start each session. The arrival activities are designed to give people something worthwhile and engaging to do as soon as they arrive, without having to wait for stragglers. They may even prompt people to be on time! The suggested activities encourage people to get better acquainted with each other and begin to focus their attention on the topic for the session.

As you prepare for this course, gather a collection of "angels." These may be craft projects, Christmas ornaments, art prints, Christmas cards, or illustrations. You might use them to decorate your meeting room for the duration of the program. You could invite people to bring their own angel items to share with the group. For this session, you will need to have your angel items set up before the first person comes into the room.

As people come in, they will be naturally drawn to look at the angel items you have on display. Encourage them to talk informally with each other by answering the questions you have written on a sheet of newsprint and posted where they can easily be seen as people enter:

- What features do the different angels have in common?

- What unique qualities do certain of the angels have?

- Which angels do you find most appealing? Why?

- In what ways are these angels similar to and different from the angels you know about in the Bible?

Greet people as they enter, introducing yourself and inviting them to engage in conversation about the angels in the room. Have chairs set up in advance so you can begin promptly at starting time. Begin by welcoming people to this course and formally introducing yourself. Then lead the group in prayer, asking for God's presence and direction today and in the weeks ahead as you investigate and discuss the topic of angels.

IMAGINATIVE EXPLORATION
10-15 minutes

Explain that this is a course on what the Bible teaches about angels, and that it will give everyone the opportunity to compare the Bible's teachings with many of the popular and sometimes bizarre ideas people have about angels. Hold up a copy of *In the Company of Angels* and say a little about your impressions of the book as you read it to prepare for the course. Let the group know it will be the text and study guide for this course, and that you will distribute copies at the end of this first session.

Generally, each session begins with an activity that relates to the interest and experience of group members. Christians and non-Christians alike are intrigued by angels. We human beings enjoy probing mysteries and speculating, sometimes fancifully, about them. Both believers and unbelievers long for contact with the holy, the awesome. This longing can draw us to a deeper fellowship with God, or it can entice us into dangerous pursuits. Thus, each session begins with an activity that captures our imagination and inspires us to pursue the dependable work of God.

Move into the first learning activity by saying something like this to the group:

> "Angels have become very popular subjects for books, movies and TV shows, personal groups, and even national organizations. As you came in, you looked at and talked about a variety of images of angels. Some of these bear little, if any, resemblance to the angels whose meetings with people are recorded in the Bible. In just a few minutes we'll be looking at some of the encounters between people and angels reported in the Bible. But first, let's talk about imaginative influences on our ideas about angels."

Read the following imaginative description of angels to the group. Alert group members to think of how this fanciful conception of angels is different from the more common portraits around the room.

He had met the creatures called *eldila,* and specially that great eldil who is the ruler of Mars or, in their speech, the *Oyarsa* of *Malacandra.* The eldila are very different from any planetary creatures. Their physical organism, if organism it can be called, is quite unlike either the human or the Martian. They do not eat, breed, breathe, or suffer natural death, and to that extent resemble thinking minerals more than they resemble anything we should recognize as an animal. Though they appear on planets and may even seem to our senses to be sometimes resident in them, the precise spatial location of an eldil at any moment presents great problems. They themselves regard space (of "Deep Heaven") as their true habitat, and the planets are to them not closed worlds but merely moving points—perhaps even interruptions—in what we know as the Solar System and they as the Field of Arbol.

C. S. Lewis, *Perelandra,* New York: Macmillan, 1965, © 1944.

Start a discussion of popular ideas and images of angels by asking these questions:

1. How would the average person in your neighborhood describe angels?

2. What prompts people to think of angels in feminine, sentimental, and even childlike ways?

3. How do such concepts influence what comes into our minds when we read about angels in the Bible?

REALITY CHECK
20-30 minutes

The learning activity at the center of each session is a reality check with the Bible. The Bible is the only reliable, authoritative measure by which all matters of faith and life can be evaluated. So what we believe about angels or any other spiritual creatures must be subjected to the test of Scripture. Otherwise our faith and life in Christ is endangered.

This course will give your group opportunities to examine theology, philosophy, mystical insights, imaginative literature, creative speculation, and the experiences of others, along with the personal experiences of people in the group. All of these will be held up against the Bible for a reality check. The Bible is the only reliable guide in knowing about the spiritual reality this course will examine. *In the Company of Angels* will help you find the relevant material in the Bible and analyze its significance for the issues and questions this course probes.

In this first session's Reality Check, your group will develop a composite "angel portrait" based on some angel encounters that are recorded in the Bible. Divide into eight subgroups with two to five people in each group. If your group has less than sixteen people, double up on assignments so each group has two incidents to examine. Keep at least two people in each group so they will get the benefit of interacting with each other. If your group is larger than about forty, form sixteen subgroups and give one assignment to two groups. That way the subgroups will stay small enough that everyone will be able to participate fully.

The group assignments follow:

Group One	*Moses*	Exodus 3:1-6
Group Two	*Balaam*	Numbers 22:21-34
Group Three	*Gideon*	Judges 6:20-22
Group Four	*Manoah*	Judges 13:17-22
Group Five	*Guards at Jesus' tomb*	Matthew 28:2-5
Group Six	*Zechariah*	Luke 1:8-22
Group Seven	*Mary*	Luke 1:26-30
Group Eight	*Shepherds*	Luke 2:8-10

Instruct the subgroups to carefully examine their assigned Scripture passages. They should try to put themselves in the place of the person who meets the angel or angels. Using only the material in the passage, each group is to describe the angel. These may be descriptions of spiritual or personal qualities or attributes rather than physical characteristics. These qualities may be deduced from the reaction of the person encountered by the angel as well as by direct description in the text. Ask the subgroups to record their findings to share with the whole group.

After the subgroups have had a chance to work, call the whole group together and prepare a composite "angel portrait": a written list of the qualities of angels apparent from reading the stories in the Bible of those who encountered angels. Ask one person from each group to report what they found in the passage they examined. As they report, record the insights on sheets of newsprint. As you fill each sheet of paper, post it with masking tape where it will be visible for the rest of the session. You may wish to refer back to these sheets in session 3, when you will investigate chapter 2 of *In the Company of Angels*.

When all the subgroups have reported, review your composite portrait of angels. Compare and contrast this portrait with the other representations of angels you

discussed at the beginning of this session by asking these questions:

1. Of the popular images of angels, what is consistent with the picture you have compiled from the Bible?

2. Of these popular images, what is inconsistent with what you discovered in the Bible?

3. What seem to be the most important realities about angels in the experiences of those who encountered angels in the Bible?

PERSONAL CONNECTION
10-15 minutes

The apostle Paul reminds us that "all Scripture . . . is useful" (2 Tim. 3:16). This course on angels has a greater significance than satisfying our curiosity, though the desire to learn and to understand are good and important dimensions of how humans are created in God's image. It assumes that when people examine God's Word in good faith, they will receive real benefits. Thus, each session ends with an activity to help people make practical, personal connections between what they are learning and their own lives.

People are better motivated to learn, to study, to participate and to connect the truth of God's Word to their personal experience when they know that they will be covering things of interest and value to them. By listing these expectations at the beginning of the course and recording when they are covered, people will have a sense of accomplishment and progress as the course develops. They will also gain an appreciation of the needs and interests of others.

To achieve these benefits for the people in your group, ask them: "What questions would you like to have answered as we proceed with this study of angels?" Write their questions on sheets of newsprint; then post the sheets for everyone to see.

You will want to keep these sheets posted throughout the course. As each question is covered, mark it off. One way to do this is to write the date you covered an item in a contrasting color marker in the right margin alongside the item. Do this as part of the group process. As you mark it off, ask the group, "Did we handle this adequately?" In some cases, of course, fully satisfying answers may not be available. That is all right, as long as you acknowledge it.

The list of questions can also help you as leader customize this course for your group. Reread *In the Company of Angels* with the list at hand. Try to identify the chapter in which it would be most logical to address each question and issue. Write that number in a contrasting color in the left margin. In some cases, a direct fit may not be possible—in that case, make the most logical connection you can. Your aim is to respond to each item by the end of the course.

Before dismissing people, distribute copies of *In the Company of Angels*. Ask them to read chapter 1, "Why Study about Angels?" before the next session so they will be able to contribute to the discussion. Also encourage them to read chapters 1 and 2 of Hebrews. That section contains the most complete information about angels in one place in the Bible. It will be the basis for next session's Reality Check and will be referred to again during the course. Familiarity with this passage will give a solid foundation for understanding the Bible's teachings about angels and evaluating other input about angels.

Conclude with a prayer asking God to illumine people's hearts by the Holy Spirit so they will be able to understand God's Word and discern truth when confronting various teachings about angels. Also, ask God to make his Word about angels useful to group members in living out their faith in Christ.

Remind everyone to bring *In the Company of Angels* to each group meeting.

WHY STUDY ABOUT ANGELS?

SESSION GOALS

- to establish the principles of study that are followed in this course

- to define the goals for the course in terms of gaining strength for spiritual struggle

- to share personal experiences that may be connected to angels in some fashion

- to lay a foundation of biblical teaching on angels from Hebrews 1-2 that will be used throughout the course

MATERIALS

- Bibles for all participants (encourage them to bring their own)

- *In the Company of Angels* (participants should bring their own copy; bring a couple of extra copies for newcomers)

- Hospitality table supplies

- Newsprint pad

- Newsprint with categories of angel stories (see Imaginative Exploration)

- Markers

- Masking tape

- Notebook for group prayer list

ARRIVAL ACTIVITY

As people begin to arrive for this second session, greet them and point out the question you have written on a sheet of newsprint or on a chalkboard for all to see: "Why study about angels?" Ask people to jot down their reasons on the newsprint or on your chalkboard. After everyone in your group has had a chance to list their reasons, you may want to compare them to the ones Andrew Bandstra gives in his book:

1. It is safer than studying demons.

2. It helps us understand God's power.

3. It makes us biblically informed.

To begin the session, call everyone together. Let them know that one of the powerful benefits of a group that stays together for several sessions to study the Bible is getting to know and care for each other. Introduce the idea of caring and praying for each other by inviting those who have specific concerns to share them at this time. Tell them that you will pray for them during the week, and encourage them to do the same for each other. Write the prayer concerns in a small notebook, which you can use to remember to pray for those in your group. Then lead in prayer, mentioning the specific requests briefly.

IMAGINATIVE EXPLORATION
10-15 minutes

In this step, you will be encouraging group members to share their "angel stories"—that is, any personal experience people have had that they think might have involved angels.

Prior to today's session, list on a sheet of newsprint list the following categories:

- stories in which angels seem to be conveying some sort of message from God

- stories in which angels worship God

- stories in which angels guard or protect believers

- stories in which angels encourage obedience to God

- stories in which angels administer God's justice

Assure group members that they do not have to be certain angels were involved, only that they wondered if angels were involved. If some people have not had a personal "angel experience," they may tell about an experience they have heard from a relative, friend, or neighbor. These incidents do not have to be dramatic or bizarre. The point is not to come to conclusions about what the experiences mean, but to encourage people to share them with each other.

After each person who wants to has shared an "angel story," ask the group to decide which category the story falls under. Tell the group that in the sessions ahead they will be examining what the Bible says about these specific functions of angels, which should help people understand their experiences.

REALITY CHECK
20-30 minutes

Hebrews 1-2 brings together in one place more specific information about angels than any other section of Scripture. The point of Hebrews 1-2 is really to tell us about Jesus Christ, but along the way it tells us a lot about angels and human beings too.

To examine this passage, divide into three subgroups. Give each subgroup a sheet or two of newsprint and a marker. One group will look for qualities that describe Jesus Christ, another for qualities that describe human beings, and the third for qualities that describe angels. Each group is to list on newsprint the qualities they find.

After the groups have finished, a representative of each group should read the lists to the whole group and post them for everyone to see. Then lead a group discussion using some of the following questions:

1. In what ways are angels similar to and different from human beings?

2. In what ways are angels similar to and different from Jesus Christ?

3. What guidance can this passage give us for pursuing our study of angels?

4. How does the centrality of Jesus Christ in this passage help us evaluate reports of angel experiences or teachings about angels from non-Christian sources?

5. What can you conclude about the significance of angels from this passage?

This passage has the most foundational and comprehensive material on angels in the Bible. If you are intrigued by angels, become thoroughly familiar with Hebrews 1-2. It is the place to look for biblical principles when discussing angels with someone who is coming at the subject from a non-biblical perspective. It is the compass to consult when you read an exciting book or see a film or television program that claims to have some special insights into angels. It will help you integrate all of the other things you will learn about angels.

PERSONAL CONNECTION
10-15 minutes

In his book, Andrew Bandstra refers to John Calvin's reminder not to fall into speculation or superstition but to seek what is true, sure, profitable, and beneficial. In the same vein, Karl Barth encourages us to speak of angels "softly and incidentally." These principles are evident in Bandstra's writing and have also guided the preparation of this leader's guide. Present these principles to the group, asking them to discuss the advantages and limitations of such an approach.

Assure the group that there will be opportunities to talk about popular, even non-Christian, input on angels and to explore personal "angel experiences." The point of following such careful principles is not to quash the enjoyment of the experience nor to stifle the group. Rather, it is to enable the group to respond to the full range of ideas about angels in a reliable way that guarantees real direction, not just a patchwork of subjective, unrelated, and maybe inconsistent opinions.

Scripture leaves plenty of room for creativity and imagination. And it is certainly true that to wonder in the face of a mystery is healthy. As a leader you can nourish this wonder and awe as you guide people in studying about angels. However, to begin treating our musings and questions as though they were answers is to venture into dangerous territory, especially when it comes to spiritual reality. So these careful principles for study are not so much a restriction as a structure that offers freedom to probe any question without fear.

Encourage people to read chapter 2, "What Angels Are Like," for the next session. Several people in the group have likely done some reading about angels from New Age or other non-Christian sources. Ask if those persons would bring in a brief selection that they find particularly significant to be read and reviewed at the next session. They may wish to compare the selection with Hebrews 1-2 ahead of time.

Ask someone in the group to close the session with prayer. He or she may include the prayer concerns named at the start of the session. This will begin to get the group used to having a variety of people pray, which can set the stage for praying for each other.

WHAT ANGELS ARE LIKE

SESSION GOALS

- to be able to distinguish biblical characteristics of angels from fanciful speculation

- to adopt an accurate biblical picture of what angels are like

- to explore what is beneficial for Christian believers in this generation to know about the nature of angels

MATERIALS

- Quotes about angels from New Age or other non-biblical sources (you may want to photocopy page 15 for each participant)

- Composite portrait of angels from session 1

- Table for displaying books, magazines, etc. about angels

- Bibles for all participants (encourage them to bring their own)

- Hospitality table supplies

- Newsprint pad

- Markers

- Masking tape

- Notebook for recording prayer concerns

- *In the Company of Angels* (participants should bring their own copies; bring a couple of extra copies for newcomers)

ARRIVAL ACTIVITY

Set up a table in advance to display your own collection of popular New Age or other non-biblical books and articles on angels, to supplement what people in the group will bring. As people arrive with their own items, ask them to add the items to the table. They may want to have their names written on slips of paper clipped to the books, magazines, or articles. A few quotes are included in this leader's guide as examples of the kind of thing that may be suitable. You may wish to photocopy these quotes to add to your collection.

As people come in, encourage them to browse through the materials on the tables. On a sheet of newsprint or a chalkboard near the tables write this question: "What is the most outrageous, farfetched claim you have heard about angels?" That should stimulate considerable conversation.

Call the group together promptly at starting time. Give people the opportunity to mention prayer concerns, then write them in the prayer notebook. Review the prayer concerns from the last session. Then form huddles of three or four people who will take a couple of minutes to pray for the others in the group.

On page 15 ("About Angels") are some quotes you may wish to photocopy for the browsing table.

IMAGINATIVE EXPLORATION
10-15 minutes

Start by referring to the composite portrait of angels prepared in session 1. Then list on a sheet of newsprint the characteristics of angels from *In the Company of Angels:* spiritual, created, limited, holy, individualistic. Ask the group to brainstorm other possible qualities of angels. Tell them that these do not have to be biblical, accurate, or realistic. Rather, the group's task is to make a list of the attributes people assign to angels, even if these are not supported by Scripture. Make the list with only a single column of qualities on each sheet of paper, leaving space in the margin for adding notes in a contrasting color. As you fill one sheet, post it where everyone can see.

After about five minutes of brainstorming, ask the group to look over the list and evaluate the accuracy of each item. Note your group's evaluations by marking these letters in the margin:

B — for those that are clearly taught in the Bible

C — for those that are consistent with what is taught in the Bible

F — for those that are fanciful or imaginary and are not taught in the Bible

W — for those that are wrong or inconsistent with what the Bible teaches

U — for those that are unknown or about which a general consensus does not arise in your group

The idea here is not to arrive at a definitive assessment or a comprehensive list. Instead, the point is to get the group to begin to think critically and biblically about angels. Do not let the group engage in debate for items on which they do not generally agree. Simply mark them **U** and say, "We'll watch for answers to this as we look further in the Bible through this course." Respect the opinions of those who may express strongly held minority views. Again, you can defer to what you expect to emerge as the study proceeds. Letting the Bible speak for itself is probably the best way to handle dissident opinion.

Conclude this step by discussing for a few moments the sources people draw from in formulating their pictures of angels. Of course the Bible is central, but people may also mention personal experience, reports of others' experiences, art and literature, and input from other religions. Ask the group to think about and discuss the influence these different sources might have on our understanding of angels.

REALITY CHECK
20-30 Minutes

Divide into subgroups of six to eight people by combining two of the huddles that prayed together at the beginning. Each subgroup is to go back through Hebrews 1-2 and compare it with the list of characteristics of angels developed by the whole group. The subgroups will be most productive if they have a recorder to consolidate their work. The groups are to proceed by answering these questions, which you should post on a sheet of newsprint, one at a time:

1. Which qualities of angels on our list can be supported from Hebrews 1-2?

2. Which qualities of angels might be supported from other Scripture passages according to *In the Company of Angels?*

3. Which qualities of angels are refuted by Hebrews 1-2?

4. Which qualities of angels might be refuted from other passages according to *In the Company of Angels?* What evidence can you cite against them?

PERSONAL CONNECTION
10-15 minutes

Ask the subgroups to draw on their insights from the Hebrews 1-2 exercise to develop an answer to the following question: Why do you think the Bible emphasizes the characteristics of angels that it does? The groups should write out a one- or two-sentence answer on a sheet of newsprint. Ask them to post their answer as soon as they are done. That will let you know when to move on to the conclusion of this session.

When all of the subgroups have posted their answers, have one person from each read the group's answer and explain anything that is unclear. After all the groups have reported, engage in a whole group discussion.

Introduce the discussion by reminding the group of John Calvin's advice to focus on what is profitable and beneficial when studying about angels. Then ask, "From what the Bible does and does not tell us about angels, what can we conclude is profitable and beneficial for us in studying angels?" Allow the discussion to include people's responses to how profitable and beneficial pursuing fanciful speculation and personal experiences might be.

Before dismissing the group, look back at the list of questions for which people want answers. Have you covered any of them in this session? If so, be sure to mark them. Assign people to read chapter 3, "Names and Titles of Angels." Ask someone to conclude with a prayer asking God to help people discern what is profitable and beneficial as they prepare for the next session.

ABOUT ANGELS

(Allen) Duncan had been kicked off Willingboro's police force five years earlier after a near emotional collapse and a halfhearted suicide attempt.

Trying to put his life back together, Duncan turned to Zen Buddhism, a religion that teaches enlightenment through meditation and a spiritual connection to all living things.

During his daily sojourns in the park, Duncan would sit and wait for a vision of a master, or guru, to provide the insight that would help him attain enlightenment.

On that day twelve years ago, Duncan was expecting to come out of his meditative state to find a guru standing before him. Instead, he saw a young girl tossing rocks into a pond.

"At that moment, I realized I had been so serious in looking for answers to the meaning of life and all sorts of other questions . . . And when I saw the little girl was so happy just throwing rocks into the pond, it hit me that the real meaning of life was to take things lightly and just live in the moment," he said.

To Duncan, that young girl, whom he never spoke to and never saw again, was a messenger from God, or what most people would call an angel.

"Angels don't necessarily have to have wings," he said. "They are merely vehicles or middlemen that bring messages inspiring us to do good and change our lives. They can appear as anything or anyone."

Burlington County Times, Willingboro, New Jersey, October 30, 1994.

There is an uninterrupted chain in nature of increasing biological complexity and intellectual capacity. In the natural life of the earth, this chain begins at the bottom with the simplest plant organisms and works its way up through all the plant and animal species to human beings. The differences between the successive "links"—or lifeforms—in the chain are relatively small.

Because the difference between the nature of humans and God seems so great, there must necessarily be intelligent beings forming the link, or links, in the chain between humans and God. Just as humans look "down" the chain of the animal and plant species, we should also be able to look "up" at the higher beings we call angels. . . .

Several contemporary New Age angelologists have stated their belief in twelve—not seven—archangels. . . . Names of individual angels have commonly been associated with the twelve signs of the zodiac.

David Connolly, *In Search of Angels,* New York: Putnam Publishing Group, 1993.

Patti Lipman is a former anthropologist who studied the Northwest Coast Indians for the Smithsonian Institution. She always felt an affinity for crows. They can taunt you, tease you, she says. They chase away predators. They are smart and people can tame them. Crows are Patti's totem. Whenever times are bad, she looks for crows, and if she sees one, she knows everything is going to be okay. They are her angels.

One year at Vail she had a ski accident. She smashed into a tree, shattered her ribs, and occasioned nerve damage to the right elbow and hand. It was the kind of high-speed accident that is usually fatal, and every year three or four expert skiers die by slamming into trees.

After that, she was alone all day, recovering, and the pain, she says, was intolerable! She was sitting on the sofa in her condominium watching TV with a channel changer. She couldn't stand up. She was lamenting, "Why, me! Why, God, did this happen to me?"

Then she saw two crows on a nearby roof. She was surprised, for you rarely see a crow in Vail, she says. They flew to the railing of her balcony, and then clear as day she heard a voice: "But, Patti, we let you live."

Sophy Burnham, *A Book of Angels,* New York: Ballantine Books, 1990.

NAMES AND TITLES OF ANGELS

SESSION GOALS

- to further understand the nature of angels from the biblical names used for them

- to further understand the function of angels from the labels and groupings used for them in the Bible

- to distinguish the simple biblical categories of angels from the complex, imaginary organizations developed over the centuries

- to develop biblically accurate expectations for the work of angels in the world and in the lives of people

MATERIALS

- Bibles for all participants (encourage them to bring their own)

- *In the Company of Angels* (participants should bring their own copy)

- Four complete concordances

- Examples of imaginary organizational schemes for angels (you may want to photocopy page 20 for each participant)

- Hospitality table supplies

- Newsprint pad

- Markers

- Masking tape

- Notebook for recording prayer concerns

ARRIVAL ACTIVITY

On page 20 are some examples of imaginary organizational schemes for angels. We suggest you photocopy these and distribute them as people arrive.

As people mingle, ask them to discuss why such organizational schemes arose and to what extent these schemes seem to be based on Scripture. They may want to consult chapter 3 of *In the Company of Angels* for additional comments.

Call the group together promptly at starting time, and ask for prayer concerns. Write them in the prayer notebook and review the prayer concerns from the last session. Then have people form four subgroups, each of whom will take a couple of minutes to pray for each other.

IMAGINATIVE EXPLORATION

10-15 minutes

Keep people in the four subgroups, giving each group two sheets of newsprint and a marker or two. Each group should select a recorder, who will head one sheet "Benefits Believers Receive from Angels" and the other sheet "Benefits People Claim to Receive from Angels." This second heading refers to claims people make that are doubtful.

The subgroups should try to list three to five benefits on each sheet. As leader, you can circulate to see how they are doing and whether they need any assistance to get started. Possibilities for the "Benefits Believers Receive from Angels" sheet include: protection, encouragement in faith, guidance, assurance in crisis. Possibilities for the "Benefits People Claim to Receive from Angels" sheet include: knowing lottery numbers in advance, the ability to communicate with people who have died, special revelation in addition to the Bible, blending worship of different religions.

When each group has some ideas listed for both sheets, have the recorders read aloud the "Benefits Believers Receive from Angels" sheets and post them together in a cluster. Do the same thing with the "Benefits People Claim to Receive from Angels" sheets.

Analyzing and evaluating the work of the subgroups is not necessary. The goal of this exercise is to stimulate thought and direct attention to practical concerns in preparation for looking at the names and titles of angels in the Bible.

REALITY CHECK
20-30 Minutes

Continue to work in the same four subgroups. Each group will need a concordance, Bibles, another sheet of newsprint, and a marker. People will want to refer to chapter 3 of *In the Company of Angels* as well. Assign each group one of the following topics:

- Names of angels

- Titles of angels

- Groups of angels

- Descriptions of angels

Each subgroup is to examine the biblical material relevant to its assigned topic, paying special attention to how the language is used and what it tells us about the functions of angels. The groups should try to come up with a single statement describing their central conclusion. The groups may use chapter 3 of *In the Company of Angels,* a concordance, and some of these suggestions:

Names of Angels
Only two angels are actually named in the Bible: Michael, which means "Who is like God" (Jude 9; Dan. 10:13, 21; 12:1; Rev. 12:7), and Gabriel, "God is strong" (Dan. 8:16-26; 9:20-27; Luke 1). Exodus 23:21 gives some hint about the significance of names. Keeping this passage in mind, encourage the groups to see what they can observe about the function of angels from the meanings of the names Michael and Gabriel. Relate these to the biblical incidents involving these two angels.

Titles of Angels
In the Company of Angels lists several titles for angels and the Bible passages where these titles may be found. In addition, the group can use a concordance to find occurrences of these titles: sons of God, spirits, holy ones or saints, watchers. Ask the group to make observations about the functions of angels by examining the titles given to angels.

Groups of Angels
The book also lists several groups or types of angels and the Bible passages where they may be found. The group can use a concordance to find additional occurrences of these groups: cherubim, seraphim, archangels, angels, principalities, and powers. Take note that in some pas-

sages certain groups may be associated with evil rather than good. What observations can the group make about the functions of angels by investigating the different groups of angels?

Descriptions of Angels
Angels are described in a number of passages. Sometimes those who observed them did not distinguish them from humans. At other times they appeared as creatures of such light and glory that observers were struck with fear or inclined to worship. The group may look at a few of these descriptions, as well as use a concordance to pursue any others they wish. What do these descriptions suggest about the functions of angels?

After the subgroups have completed their investigations and have formulated their statements on the functions of angels, have each group report and post its statement for all to see.

PERSONAL CONNECTION
10-15 minutes

Call everyone together in a single group. Ask them to look carefully at the statements developed by the subgroups. Then lead the group in creating a kind of generic job description for angels. List these tasks and roles on newsprint.

In a way, the subsequent chapters of *In the Company of Angels* constitute a sort of job description for angels. Compare these chapter titles with the job description your group came up with. What has you group found that is not covered by these titles? What do the titles suggest that your group did not include?

- messengers of God

- those who praise God

- guardians of believers

- ministers of justice

Conclude your group session by discussing how the various functions of angels affect us as believers.

- What interactions between people and angels seem to be implied by the job description you have prepared?

- How aware do you think believers are or should be of interaction or involvement with angels?

Before dismissing people, look back at the list of questions for which people want answers. Can you mark any of them as having been covered in this session? Ask people to read chapter 4, "Messengers of God." It will also be helpful to assign people for a dramatic reading of Genesis 18 for the next session, so that people can practice and be more confident reading aloud. You will need a narrator, Abraham, the angel (of "the Lord"), and Sarah. Ask someone to conclude with a prayer asking God to help people appreciate and appropriate the redemptive message announced by angels through biblical history.

IMAGINARY ORGANIZATIONAL SCHEMES FOR ANGELS

Most organizational schemes for angels are variations of, or arguments with, what Dionysius proposed in *The Celestial Hierarchy* in the sixth century. The following is a simple outline of his scheme of organization:

Hierarchy One

    seraphim (the highest grade of perfection in God's creation)

    cherubim

    thrones

Hierarchy Two

    dominions

    virtues

    powers

Hierarchy Three

    principalities

    archangels

    angels (the lowest level of perfection in mode of being)

From Mortimer J. Adler, *The Angels and Us,*
New York: Macmillan Publishing Co., Inc., 1982.

Sophy Burnham summarizes the supposed functions of several orders of angels.

Seraphim, the highest order, the six-winged ones, surround the throne of God, singing ceaselessly, Holy, Holy, Holy. They are angels of love, light, and fire.

Cherubim are the guardians of the fixed stars, keepers of celestial records, bestowers of knowledge. In the Talmud cherubim are equated with the order of wheels, also called *ophanim.* Chief rulers are Ophaniel, Rikbiel, Zophiel, and before his fall, Satan.

Thrones bring God's justice to us. They are sometimes called *wheels* in the Jewish Kabbalah, *chariots* or the *Merkabah.* The occult book, the *Zohar,* ranks wheels above seraphim, but other sources place them as cherubim, the whole thing being confused. The ruling prince is Oriphiel or Zabkiel or Zaphiel.

Dominions or *Dominations* regulate angelic duties. Through them is manifested the Majesty of God. They hold an orb or septre as an emblem of authority, and in Hebraic lore, the chief of this order is named Hasmal or Zadkiel.

Virtues work miracles on earth. They are bestowers of grace and valor.

Powers stop the efforts of demons to overthrow the world, or else they preside over demons, or perhaps (according to St. Paul) they are themselves evil. Ertosi, Sammael, or Camael (depending on the source) is the chief of the Powers.

Principalities are protestors of religion. Misroc, in Milton, is "of principalities the prime," and others, according to various sources, are named Requel, Anael, and Cerviel.

Archangels and *Angels* are guardians of people and all physical things.

A Book of Angels, New York: Ballantine Books, 1990.

MESSENGERS OF GOD

SESSION GOALS

- to appreciate the special role of angels as God's messengers in communicating God's redemptive plans

- to explore the role of angels as God's messengers to individuals in Scripture

- to explore if and how angels might convey God's messages today

MATERIALS

- Bibles for all participants (encourage them to bring their own)

- *In the Company of Angels* (participants should bring their own copy)

- Hospitality table supplies

- Examples of claims for revelatory messages from angels

- Newsprint pad

- Markers

- Masking tape

- Notebook for recording prayer concerns

ARRIVAL ACTIVITY

As people enter the room, encourage them to talk informally with each other about what fascinates them most about angels, or what they don't understand, keeping in mind especially the biblical examples of angels as messengers of God mentioned in *In the Company of Angels*. Ask each one to mention which of these is particularly appealing or puzzling to him or her.

This informal conversation is not intended to formulate doctrine or solve exegetical problems. It should help people get better acquainted with each other and begin to think about the role of angels as messengers.

Then call the group together, encouraging people to sit near those with whom they have just been talking. Ask for prayer concerns, and write them in the prayer notebook. After reviewing the prayer concerns from the last session, ask people to pray for each other.

IMAGINATIVE EXPLORATION

10-15 minutes

In this session, your group will be examining a number of accounts from people who have claimed to have received personal revelation from God by way of an angel. According to the revelation of Scripture, God conveyed messages through angels at a number of key points in carrying through his redemptive plan: in establishing the covenant with the patriarchs, during the exodus from Egypt and the conquest of the Promised Land, at Jesus' birth and resurrection.

Perhaps stimulated by this pattern in Scripture, people who have founded new and often novel religious movements have also claimed to have received new revelation from God by way of an angel. In many cases these revelations carry messages well beyond the scope of the Bible.

Your group will examine some of these claims as a way of discerning when an angel message can be relied upon.

To conduct this discussion, explain to the group that you will be reading or telling about supposed new revelations given by angels. After each one, you will ask the group to discuss it by asking, "What's wrong with this picture? That is, what makes this different from the revelations delivered by angels in the Bible, and what does that mean for this claim?" The idea is to help people recognize differences between biblical and non-biblical accounts of angel messages.

Ask the group to keep in mind a few key passages from the apostle Paul for guidance. Perhaps you would find it helpful to write them on a piece of newsprint and post it where everyone can see.

- Galatians 1:8: Even if we or an angel from heaven should preach a gospel other than the one we preached to you, let him be eternally condemned!

- Romans 8:38-39: For I am convinced that . . . neither angels nor demons . . . will be able to separate us from the love of God that is in Christ Jesus our Lord.

- 2 Corinthians 11:14: Satan himself masquerades as an angel of light.

You may wish to make your own collection of non-biblical messages that have claimed to have been God's revelation through angels, or you can draw on the examples listed here.

> I was shown that This Spirit, or This Immense, Creative Being was literally in everything. There was so much love and care in everything that it cannot be expressed in words. It's beyond the walls of towns, countries, nations; it's larger than any rabbi, priest, saint. I saw that Mankind wants to follow his interpretation, but that the Spirit of Love knows absolutely No Bounds. It loves Buddhists, Taoists, Jews, Moslems, and on and on and on with incredible Love. . . . Man wants to "own God," and says that God sees only one group as great and everyone else as wrong. . . . I saw what This Spirit sees. . . . No need to compete, destroy, be disillusioned, Just total contentment, peace with self, with others, the environment. . . . I guess the most important thing I could say about it is that how one thinks directs one's path and one's path directs him or her forever.
>
> Susan Callas, in Sophy Burnham, *A Book of Angels*, New York: Ballantine Books, 1990.

In September of 1979 my guardian angel and certain other angels who serve God with him began to teach me a number of things about the way their society is organized and the nature and abilities of angels. . . . I kept my "journal" and my meditations regularly. By the time Enniss (my guardian angel) told me that the initial work was finished, it had become a four-volume, twelve-hundred-page work that I named *The Guardians of the Earth*. I divided it into four volumes based on periods of unusually strong insights I had received: *The Pilot Program*, in which Enniss describes a new sort of relationship that is now beginning to develop between angels and humans; *The House of Healing*, which shows how we can work through the medium of God's grace to heal our lives of evil and darkness; *The Rituals of God*, which explores the ways heaven and earth are growing closer together as this present age winds down; and *The*

Percivale Riddle, which envisions a world in which angels and humans cooperate in a new and stronger way than ever before to transform this world.

Eileen Elias Freeman, *Touched by Angels*, New York: Warner Books, 1993.

I wanted to know why there were so many churches in the world. Why didn't God give us only one church, one pure religion? The answer came to me with the purest of understanding. Each of us, I was told, is at a different level of spiritual development and understanding. Each person is therefore prepared for a different level of spiritual knowledge. All religions upon the earth are necessary because there are people who need what they teach. People in one religion may not have a complete understanding of the Lord's gospel and never will have while in that religion. But that religion is a stepping stone to further knowledge. Each church fulfills spiritual needs that perhaps others cannot fill. No one church can fulfill everybody's needs at every level. As an individual raises his level about God and his own eternal progress, he might feel discontented with the teachings of his present church and seek a different philosophy or religion to fill that void. When this occurs he has reached another level of understanding and will long for further truth and knowledge, and for another opportunity to grow. And at every step of the way, these new opportunities to learn will be given.

Having received this knowledge, I knew that we have no right to criticize any church or religion in any way. They are all precious and important in his sight. Very special people with important missions have been placed in all countries, in all religions, in every station of life, that they might touch others. . . .

All people as spirits in the pre-mortal world took part in the creation of the earth. We were thrilled to be part of it. We were with God, and we knew that he created us, that we were his very own children. He was pleased with our development and was filled with absolute love for each one of us. Also, Jesus Christ was there. I understood, to my surprise, that Jesus was a separate being from God, with his own divine purpose, and I knew that God was our mutual Father.

Betty Eadie, *Embraced by the Light*, Placerville, CA: Gold Leaf Press, 1992.

The angel Moroni gave Joseph Smith instructions for finding and translating the Book of Mormon, which filled in missing information from the Bible and inspired the founding of the Church of Jesus Christ of the Latter-day Saints (the Mormons) to purify and correct the corruptions of Christianity.

After discussing each of the examples you have selected, return to the passages from the Bible you quoted earlier and discuss the following:

- With the closing of the New Testament cannon, the church does not expect any further revelation or addition to the Bible. Does that mean that we should not expect angels to serve as God's messengers to humans in our generation?

- If angels do serve as God's messengers in our generation but their messages are not additions to the revelation of Scripture, what sorts of messages might we expect them to convey?

You will return to this discussion in the conclusion of this session.

REALITY CHECK
20-30 minutes

Genesis 18 is a case study of angels delivering God's message to a human. Read the whole chapter aloud as a dramatic reading. You will need a narrator, Abraham, the angel (also the lines for "the Lord"), and Sarah. If you made assignments at the end of last session, call on the assigned persons to read. Having them stand and read may be most effective. After the passage has been read, use the following questions to explore what can be concluded about angels as God's messengers from this case study:

1. What messages are conveyed in this incident? What priorities of importance can you assign to them?

2. Which messages are essential to God's redemptive plan for the whole human race? Which messages are for the people in that specific situation?

3. What relationships can you identify between these different kinds of messages? What can you tell about what is important to God from these messages?

4. How did Abraham recognize that these messengers were communicating God's message?

PERSONAL CONNECTION
10-15 minutes

To conclude this session, divide into seven subgroups of at least two people. Give each group a sheet of newsprint

for recording conclusions. (If you have fewer than fourteen people in your whole group, you will need to double up on assignments in order to cover all of the material.)

Assign each subgroup one of the messages to the angels of the seven churches of Asia Minor (Rev. 2-3). While the identity of the angels of these churches is uncertain, these messages can serve as a guide for the kinds of messages the church can expect from God as we wait for Jesus' return.

On a sheet of newsprint or on a chalkboard, write the following questions for each group to answer as it examines its assigned passage.

- What kinds of people are receiving this message?

- What is the nature of the message?

- What effect is the message supposed to have on those who receive it?

- What principles can be extracted from this message for evaluating messages people claim to have received from an angel?

Each group should record its findings on a sheet of newsprint and post the sheet for all to see. Then return to the discussion of the kind of messages from God that might be conveyed by angels today.

- Between the passages from the apostle Paul read earlier (Gal. 1:8; Rom. 8:38-39; 2 Cor. 11:14) and the observations made in Revelation 2-3, what might Christians today expect by way of messages from God?

- How should we evaluate and respond to people's assertions that they have received messages from angels?

This discussion can be a difficult one to bring to a fully satisfying conclusion. Certainly the purpose of angelic messages is not personal ecstasy. Any angel message that is authentic would be consistent with the Bible and affirm the redemptive message of the Gospel. Such messages would encourage righteous living and confront threats to the peace, unity, and purity of the church. Messages that claim to add to or correct the Bible can be judged fraudulent.

Before dismissing people, look back at the list of questions for which people want answers. Can you mark any of them as having been covered in this session? For next time, ask people to read chapter 5, "Those Who Praise God."

You should look over the Arrival Activity for session 6 in advance. If your group is large enough to form more than one circle of eight to twelve people, you may want to appoint conversation-starter leaders for the next session. Have them stay with you for about five minutes to get instructions (see Arrival Activity, session 6). Remind them that they should make sure they arrive early for the next session.

Ask someone to conclude with a prayer asking God to inspire their praise and motivate them to worship as they prepare for the next session.

THOSE WHO PRAISE GOD

SESSION GOALS

- to compare and contrast our worship with that of angels

- to be inspired to worship God by the worship of angels

- to learn to worship more effectively by the example of the worship of angels

MATERIALS

- Bibles for all participants (encourage them to bring their own)

- *In the Company of Angels* (participants should bring their own copy)

- Hospitality table supplies

- Newsprint pad

- Markers

- Masking tape

- Notebook for recording prayer concerns

ARRIVAL ACTIVITY

If you expect about a dozen people or less for your group, set up your chairs in advance in a circle for conversation. If your group is larger, set up circles of eight to twelve chairs around the room. You will be working in these circles throughout the session. When people come in, ask them to join a circle after helping themselves to a snack from the hospitality table. You will need one conversation-starter leader for each circle.

Ask people in the circles to tell each other about some of their most memorable or peak worship experiences. People might mention special holiday services such as Christmas Eve, Good Friday, or Easter. Others may tell about a special celebration of the Lord's Supper. Sometimes important turning points in people's lives are occasions for powerful worship experiences: baptisms, weddings, or funerals. Some folk find that particular settings particularly enable them to worship: outdoors, in cathedrals, with choirs. Whatever the setting, ask people to explain how they sensed God's presence and what drew them into deeper worship on this particular occasion.

Ask people whether they were aware of any angel participation in the worship experience they are thinking of. In retrospect, do they now think that angels might have been involved?

After people have had time to discuss their worship experiences, ask for prayer concerns and write them in the prayer notebook. Review the prayer concerns from the last session. Then let people know that you will be taking an extended time to pray at the end of this session. They may want to take some notes for themselves to be used then. Ask one person in each circle, probably the conversation-starter leader if you have appointed one, to open the formal session with prayer, asking God to guide this session.

IMAGINATIVE EXPLORATION

5-10 minutes

For this step, people can continue to stay in their circle(s). Give someone in each circle a sheet of newsprint and a marker, and ask that person to write the following sentence starter on the sheet: "Ideally, our worship should be . . ." Each group should brainstorm a list of words to complete the sentence on the sheet. Possibilities include celebrative, dignified, Christ-centered, Spirit-filled, and so on. Mention a couple of suggestions if the groups need help getting started. This exercise builds on the arrival activity by continuing to focus people's attention on worship—what it is and what we'd like it to be. When the circle(s) have finished their sheets, post them for everyone to see. People will be using their ideas about worship later in the session when they are asked to compare angel worship with human worship.

REALITY CHECK

25-30 minutes

This time, each circle will need two recorders. The recorders should each be given a sheet of newsprint and a marker. One sheet is to be headed "Similarities between Human and Angel Worship" and the other "Differences between Human and Angel Worship."

The passages listed below describe worship by angels. Using what they already know about worship, people should try to determine if the features of angel worship described in each passage are similar to or different than human worship. Each circle should work through the passages, looking for observations to list on both sheets of newsprint.

• Psalm 148

• Isaiah 6:1-7

• Luke 2:13-14

• Revelation 4:8; 5:9, 12; 7:11-12; 14:1; 15:1-3; 19

When the circle(s) are finished, call everyone together to review the lists of similarities and differences. Then discuss the following question: What can we learn from angels that would help us in our own worship? As leader, you may use the following questions as needed to stimulate discussion and keep it on track.

1. What facts about God are expressed in the angels' worship that we can include in our worship?

2. What means do the angels use to express their worship that we humans can emulate in our worship (for example, visual, vocal, symbolic, musical)?

3. What mood or emotional atmosphere do you detect in the angels' worship that would be suitable in our worship?

4. What sequences or orders of worship can you discern in the angels' worship that can be followed in our worship?

5. What motivations seem to evoke the angels' worship that would also move us to worship?

PERSONAL CONNECTION
5-10 minutes

As you told the group at the beginning of this session, you will be ending with an extended prayer time. Before the prayer time, look back at the list of questions for which people want answers. Have any of them been covered in this session? Be sure to mark them off. For next week, ask people to read chapter 6, "Guardians of Believers."

You are now almost halfway through this course. By this time, people in your group are probably feeling comfortable with praying for each other's personal concerns. This prayer time will give them a more extended opportunity to pray for each other. If your group was divided into more than one circle for most of this session, it would be good to form those circles again. Each circle will conclude its own prayer. Those that finish first should leave quietly without disturbing those who are still praying.

You will want to review your group's prayer experience so far in the course. Be sure to go over the prayer concerns that were shared at the start of this session as well. The plan for this prayer time is to blend these personal concerns with the insights gained by looking at how angels worship God. Encourage the group(s) to begin their prayer time with expressions of praise for God. As they become aware of God's reality, character, and presence, they can bring their thanks and concerns. By beginning our prayer with a focus on God, we gain God's perspective on our own situations.

GUARDIANS OF BELIEVERS

SESSION GOALS

- to clarify biblical teaching about the protecting and guarding roles of angels and to distinguish them from folklore

- to wrestle with why some believers seem to be protected in some situations and others are not

- to affirm the believer's security in God's care, even in the face of apparent disaster

MATERIALS

- Bibles for all participants (encourage them to bring their own)

- *In the Company of Angels* (participants should bring their own copy)

- Hospitality table supplies

- Newsprint pad

- Markers

- List of questions written on newsprint or chalkboard for Imaginative Exploration activity

- Masking tape

- Notebook for recording prayer concerns

ARRIVAL ACTIVITY

Before people begin to arrive, write on a chalkboard or newsprint pad: "What stories have you heard or read from Christians you respect about guardian angels?" As people arrive, ask them to share their stories in small groups. Let them know that they will have a chance to talk about their own guardian angel stories and ideas in just a few minutes, so at this time they should focus on what they have heard or read from other Christians.

When you are ready to begin the session, call the group together and give people a chance to mention prayer concerns. Write them in the prayer notebook and review the prayer concerns from the last session. Then ask people to pray for each other in small groups of three to five.

IMAGINATIVE EXPLORATION
10-15 minutes

In this activity, people will be telling about their own experiences of being protected by guardian angels. It's important that all participants have the opportunity to share their stories, so if you have more than about a dozen people, you may need to divide your group.

Many people have a "guardian angel" story to tell: an experience of escaping danger that they attribute to a guardian angel. In fact, the subject of guardian angels is probably the most popular topic in any discussion of angels. It is very likely that telling and hearing these accounts is one of the reasons some people have for participating in this course. You can probably expect enthusiastic participation.

This is not the time for biblical analysis and evaluation—that will come later in the session. The purpose of this discussion is personal sharing. Therefore, people should feel free to talk about their experiences and ideas.

In the event that someone tells something that seems far afield, as leader you can still thank them for contributing. Resist the temptation to correct things that are said in a personal sharing time. And when you get to the Bible investigation part of this session, let the Bible speak for itself. That will help keep you out of personal conflicts and shows respect for the authority and power of Scripture.

To begin the discussion, ask the following questions (prior to today's session it may be helpful to write them on the board or on a piece of newsprint). Tell people that the more of these questions they can answer in their response, the more interesting and valuable their input will be.

1. Have you ever felt you were protected by an angel? Tell about the experience.

2. What made you think that an angel might be involved? Would you distinguish the work of an angel from God's general protecting providence or the promptings of the Holy Spirit?

3. Why do you think you were protected at this particular time? Have you had other experiences of needing help when no guardian angel became involved?

4. What new perspectives did this experience give you? How did it affect your spiritual growth? In what ways have you changed your lifestyle or activities as a result?

REALITY CHECK
20-30 minutes

Although the topic of guardian angels is one on which many people have strong feelings, the Bible does not offer much specific information. This chapter of *In the Company of Angels* lists a number of Scripture passages that may have given rise to ideas about guardian angels. In this exercise, your group will looking at those passages to determine what the Bible says and does not say about guardian angels.

The relevant passages are grouped together here with questions you may use to guide your group's discussion. Refer to *In the Company of Angels* to help understand these texts. To focus your discussion, tell the group that for each of the passages we will be trying to answer the question, "What can we confidently conclude from the Bible about guardian angels?" Write your conclusions on sheets of newsprint, posting each sheet as it is filled to be seen as the discussion progresses.

- **Psalm 91:11-12** is a foundational passage for understanding the guarding role of angels. (**Psalm 34:7** uses a different metaphor to present the same principle of protection.) Read this passage as well as the two places in the New Testament where it is quoted when Satan tempts Jesus (**Matthew 4:6; Luke 4:10-11**). What is actually promised in the text? How does Satan misuse it? What is distinctly messianic about the way this is used in Scripture?

- **Exodus 23:20-23; 32:34** God sends an angel (or angels) to lead the children of Israel out of Egypt into the Promised Land. From what you know about this time in Israel's history, in what ways might the angel have protected the Israelites during the time of the exodus from Egypt and the forty years of wandering? Do any of these ways apply to the circumstances of the contemporary church?

- **Matthew 18:10** The idea of special, multiple angels assigned to children appears to be based more on sentimentality (and perhaps parental anxiety and gratitude) than on sound interpretation of the text. Read the passage and the section about it from *In the Company of*

Angels (pp. 67-8) suggesting that the "little ones" more likely refers to humble believers than children.

- A number of incidents in Scripture mention angels protecting individuals or God's people as a whole. What conclusions can you make about guardian angels for today?

    Genesis 19:15-17 Lot escapes Sodom's destruction

    2 Kings 6:8-23 Elisha and the Arameans

    Daniel 3:28 The Hebrews in the fiery furnace

    Daniel 6:22 Daniel in the lions' den

    Acts 12:7-11, 15 Peter's escape from prison

    Acts 27:23 Paul survives shipwreck

Conclude the discussion by asking, "How do our conclusions differ from popular ideas about guardian angels? What biblical evidence have we found for some of the ideas people have about guardian angels?"

PERSONAL CONNECTION
10-15 minutes

The idea of guardian angels may be comforting, but it also raises a troubling question: What about those who are not spared from harm or disaster? Often the protection of timing—missing a plane that crashes, being delayed and thereby avoiding an auto accident—means that others become victims of these tragedies. Where were their guardian angels? Or does God have some greater scheme, and, if that is the case, how can we discover it?

In *A Book of Angels,* Sophy Burnham reports the 1971 experience of Sara Michaels that raises this exact question. You may wish to read it to start this discussion.

Ten minutes from the village is a rope footbridge over a canal, lit by a bare lightbulb, and this side of it a cemetery. . . . "Okay, so it's a graveyard," I said to myself. "Don't get spooked," I said, knowing I was spooking myself all this trip.

Suddenly I heard a scream. I froze, it was so horrible. Have you ever heard two cats mating? Thinking about it afterward, I think the only sound it could have been was wildcats mating. It was eerie. It was pure evil. It scared me still. I was frozen to the road. I literally couldn't move.

"In the name of Christ, save me," I began repeating like a mantra. "In the name of Christ, save me. In the name of Christ, save me. . . . "

I'll call it "he," but I never saw anything. I didn't see anybody. He came down from up above and lifted me under each arm. He lifted me off the ground about six inches and carried me to the bridge with the lightbulb and carried me over the bridge. . . .

It was as if your mother picks you up as a child. As soothing as that.

Then he dropped me. On the other side of the bridge . . .

[My friends] looked at me. "What in the world is the matter with you?" they said.

"Just fix me some coffee," I said. "I got scared out there, but I'm alright now."

There was one girl . . . [who] kept insisting, "You have to tell me. You saw God out there."

I just looked at her.

She said, "When you came in, the light about you was so bright we couldn't look at you."

I asked Sara if she had ever seen her guardian angel since.

"No." She had told a minister at her church when she got home. His response was, "Don't tell people. It needs to be private." . . .

It's been important to Sara to tell her story, and to tell people also that since then terrible things have happened to her, and she has not been protected nor felt directed or guided in any way.

In September, 1983, for example, she was raped. Tied, bound, a knife at her throat, she kept waiting for her angel to appear, fully expecting him . . . and he didn't. He didn't save her. She puzzled over that. Finally she accepted it, thinking perhaps the experience was needed in order for her to grow, to learn more compassion perhaps even for the rapist. "And I survived. I didn't die. Or perhaps we go through horrible events for reasons we don't know. We can't expect that every time we prick our finger we'll be saved."

Or perhaps she was helped at the cemetery from something worse than rape.

Sophy Burnham, *A Book of Angels,* New York: Ballantine Books, 1990.

Refer the group to Andrew Bandstra's exploration of this question in *In the Company of Angels.* Then ask the group to discuss their thoughts.

- How do you feel about situations where one person is spared a disaster and another suffers? What role do you see God playing in these seemingly arbitrary events?

- What light does this problem shed on your understanding of the guarding and protecting role of angels? In what sense can Christians be assured of protection?

Before dismissing the group, look back at the list of questions for which people want answers. Can you mark any of them as having been covered in this session? For next week, ask people to read chapter 7, "Those Who Encourage Obedience."

As you and your group have given attention to angels during this course, you may have come across examples of experiences people claim to have had with angels that did not seem to result in Christ-centered righteousness. Ask people to bring in examples of this for your next time together. People may bring in books or magazine articles or they may tell what they have seen on television or heard in conversations.

For today's closing prayer, it is appropriate to thank God for protection through providence as well as through angels. One good way to do this is by asking people to complete the sentence, "Thank you, God, for your protection when . . . " You may close by praying, "Merciful God, we thank you for all of these times and others of which we are not aware when you have protected us. In Jesus' name."

THOSE WHO ENCOURAGE OBEDIENCE

SESSION GOALS

- to learn how angels encourage obedience to God

- to grow in obedience to God from this deeper understanding of angels

- to practice hospitality to strangers as an essential part of a righteous lifestyle

- to cultivate a willingness to serve God, following the examples of angels

MATERIALS

- Bibles for all participants (encourage them to bring their own)

- *In the Company of Angels* (participants should bring their own copy)

- Hospitality table supplies

- Examples of reports of angel encounters that did not result in obedience to God (you may want to photocopy page 33 for each participant)

- List of questions written on newsprint or chalkboard for Imaginative Exploration and Reality Check activities

- Newsprint pad

- Markers

- Masking tape

- Notebook for recording prayer concerns

ARRIVAL ACTIVITY

Popular reports of encounters with angels do not always seem to encourage an other-directed lifestyle of righteousness. Instead they may reinforce a self-centered ethos built around the pursuit and enjoyment of esoteric experiences. At the close of the last session, you asked your group to bring with them examples of experiences people claim to have had with angels that did not seem to result in Christ-centered righteousness. For this Arrival Activity you will be looking at these examples as a prelude to examining how angels work to encourage obedience to God.

As people arrive, ask them if they brought any examples of angel encounters that did not encourage obedience to God. Ask those who did to share them with others. Encourage them to discuss the examples informally, deciding how each fails to encourage obedience to God.

You should have your own examples ready to stimulate the discussion process. Some are printed on page 33 for you to photocopy and distribute, if you wish.

After people have had time to share and discuss their angel examples, call the group together and ask for prayer concerns. Write them in the prayer notebook, then review the prayer concerns from the last session. Ask people to form subgroups of four to six persons who will take a couple of minutes to pray for each other.

IMAGINATIVE EXPLORATION
10-15 minutes

Have each of the subgroups that formed for prayer select a leader to read Hebrews 13:2 and the quote from John Calvin in the text: "If anyone objects that this was an unusual occurrence [with regard to Abraham and Lot], I have a ready answer in the fact that we receive not only angels but Christ Himself when we receive the poor in His Name." Ask the leaders of each subgroup to discuss, using the following questions as a guide (have them written on your chalkboard or on newsprint ahead of time).

1. Have you ever helped a stranger that you later thought might have been an angel?

2. What clues made you suspect this?

3. What seemed to be the purpose of this encounter?

4. How do you react to Calvin's comment on Hebrews 13:2? In what ways do we receive not only angels but Christ himself when we receive the poor in his name?

REALITY CHECK
20-30 minutes

In a few places, Scripture hints that we human believers are on exhibition before the angels (1 Cor. 4:9; 11:10). Perhaps this is part of what is behind what the Bible says about entertaining angels by being hospitable to strangers. Could it be that angels are sent in disguise to believers to observe how we respond when we think no one is looking?

The Old Testament gives some examples of just such hospitality: Abraham in Genesis 18, Gideon in Judges 6 and Manoah in Judges 13. Some have even suggested that angels might be among the "great cloud of witnesses" mentioned in Hebrews 12:1, where the point clearly is to live the life of faith in Christ with vigor and faithfulness.

These passages are listed and discussed in *In the Company of Angels*. Give each subgroup a sheet or two of newsprint and a marker, and ask them to look at the passages and outline their answers to the following questions on the newsprint. Prior to your session, list the questions on newsprint or on your board. When the subgroups are finished, they can report the results to the whole group.

1. In what ways would we be more obedient to God if we were aware of being watched and maybe even cheered on by angels?

2. In what ways do these angels who observe, and maybe even visit us, encourage us to be obedient to God?

3. Would you treat strangers in a different way if you thought they might be angels in disguise?

4. In what areas of obedience do you feel you could be most helped by the encouragement of angels? How would you recognize that encouragement?

When the groups have gotten at least a page of ideas on their newsprint, have each post its sheet and summarize its findings. After all of the groups have reported, discuss with the whole group observations they can make from their findings. Were some insights unique to certain groups, or were most of the conclusions similar? What are some principles we can conclude from these discussions of Scripture? What lessons are important to pass on to others?

PERSONAL CONNECTION
10-15 minutes

Andrew Bandstra associates the third petition of the Lord's Prayer ("Your will be done on earth as it is in heaven") with the angels encouraging believers to obey God, referring to Question and Answer 124 of the Heidelberg Catechism. As a whole group, discuss people's responses to his discussion. What level of willingness to obey God is implied? What does it take to function at that level consistently?

Use this discussion to lead into a time of prayer to conclude this session. Review again the current items in your group's prayer notebook. What light does this perspective shed on the things your group is praying about right now? What new concerns does it suggest your group could be praying about?

Before the prayer, be sure to look back at the list of questions for which people want answers. Have any been covered in this session? For next week, ask people to read chapter 8, "Ministers of Justice (1)."

After taking care of these matters for next week, ask the leaders of the subgroups to gather their people again for a time of prayer that is informed by the third petition of the Lord's Prayer, "Your will be done on earth as it is in heaven." Suggest that each subgroup leader begin and end with the prayer suggested by Andrew Bandstra: "Father, help us to do your will on earth as faithfully and willingly as do the angels in heaven." In between, people can pray their own personal prayers. As each group finishes, they should leave quietly so they don't disturb others who are still praying.

ENCOUNTERS WITH ANGELS

A Mother Returns from "The Other Side"

Three times after she died, my mother came back. She was trying to tell me what it was like after death: We'd made a pact that she would try. . . .

I was lying in the pretty little canopy bed in "my" room, my childhood room, the room—the very bed—she had died in. It was ten or eleven at night. I was reading. . . .

Suddenly my mother was standing in the doorway. I looked up, saw her, and I burst into tears.

"How can I live without my mother?" I thought.

It was not her presence in the doorway that upset me, or that she had come to fulfill her pledge and tell me about The Other Side. It was that she stood there smiling at me with such unbearable love. . . .

In that moment I understood we are given physical bodies for a purpose, and we live in them like lobsters in the sea, struggling all our lives to reach outside our shells, to touch something else for some fraction of a second and transcend our isolation. . . .

I have not seen her since, though now, ten years later, I think it would be fun to try. This time maybe I'd remember to ask about death and life. But I believe that possibly we are not supposed to know. We are put here with blinkers on our eyes, to play a game of blindman's bluff with God for reasons we do not understand, and I suppose it would ruin the game if we cheated and knew the reward.

We'd never be afraid.

We'd know there's always more.

We'd want to sling ourselves into the sea of love that's God, that we glimpse on the Other Side.

And this may also be why angel visits are so rare.

Sophy Burnham, *A Book of Angels*, New York: Ballentine Books, 1990.

Expectations and Visions

The deeply religious or those spiritually inclined may or may not see visions, depending on the sect and perhaps on the openness of their hearts. But even in such circumstances we are struck by the extraordinary fact that these visitations and insights usually accord with the upbringing and conditioning of the recipient. A Hindu rarely sees a vision of Christ, and Protestants don't often dream of the Buddha, though odd to say it happens. I have a Jewish friend who, to her horror and confusion, kept witnessing Jesus Christ together with all the Christian symbolism whenever she smoked pot. Christ's face glimpsed through the darkness of a window, or a shining cross. It changed her life. I know another woman, raised an Episcopalian, who one day had so violent a vision she was termed insane. She was driving down the New Jersey Turnpike when her revelation came—Saul knocked off his horse and blinded on the road to Damascus. She was picked up by the police driving the wrong way down the road. She'd seen into other worlds, she said, and when she recovered from the resonances of her trance, she changed her dress, her diet, desires, prayers, and went to India and became a Hindu, um, priestess.

Sophy Burnham, *A Book of Angels*

Sexuality and Angels

The Islamic heaven is said to be populated by female beings called *huris,* who provide erotic delights for the male Moslems who arrive there.

Emanuael Swedenborg, himself twice rejected in earthly proposals of marriage, wrote that the angels with whom he communed married and had homes together.

David Connolly, *In Search of Angels*, New York: Putnam Publishing Co., 1993.

An Angel-Inspired Publishing Enterprise

In 1992, led, as I believe, by my own guardian angel, who I call Enniss, I started The AngelWatch Network™, a clearinghouse for all information about angels and what they are doing in today's world. I began a bimonthly magazine to keep interested individuals—angelwatchers, as I call them—up to date about angels. . . . The more information I can disseminate, the more people will begin to realize the depth of the angels' interest in us as a race and as individuals and their commitment to our growth. And the more people realize this, the more people will begin to want to work with the angels toward that end. Why, if we all become really organized in our "angel-watching," there's no telling how far the level of angel awareness on this planet might increase. With their help, we can re-create our lives, our neighborhoods, our planet.

Eileen Elias Freeman, *Touched By Angels*, New York: Time Warner, 1993.

MINISTERS OF JUSTICE (1)

SESSION GOALS

- to examine the biblical record to see how angels interact in human affairs to bring about justice

- to explore how angels might continue to be involved in human affairs to bring about justice

- to develop a balanced view of angels that includes justice as well as the more popular emphases on love and beauty

MATERIALS

- Bibles for all participants (encourage them to bring their own)

- *In the Company of Angels* (participants should bring their own copy)

- Quote for Arrival Activity

- Hospitality table supplies

- Examples of "reforming" angels in literature, film, etc.

- Newsprint pad

- Markers

- Masking tape

- Notebook for recording prayer concerns

ARRIVAL ACTIVITY

Although the role of angels as agents of God's justice is so important in the Bible that Bandstra takes two chapters in his book to cover it, popular literature about angels does not reflect that function. As people arrive, direct them to the quote from Sophy Burnham's *A Book of Angels* that you have written ahead of time on a sheet of newsprint or on your chalkboard.

[The message of angels] is always "Fear Not!" Don't worry, they say. "Things are working out perfectly. You're going to like this. Wait." Never once do you hear of an angel trumpeting bad news. . . .

Ask people to react to this popular idea about angels in informal conversation with each other.

When everyone has arrived, call the group together and invite people to mention prayer concerns. Write them in the prayer notebook and review the prayer concerns from last session. Then invite people to pray for each other in pairs. Encourage them to choose someone other than their own husband or wife as a prayer partner. You may wish to use a group of three so everyone will have someone to pray with.

IMAGINATIVE EXPLORATION
10-15 minutes

As noted in the Arrival Activity, the theme of angels as ministers of justice is noticeably absent in much of the popular literature about angels. Ask people to divide into subgroups of three to six people. Once again, ask people to avoid having spouses in the same subgroup. Tell the groups that in a few minutes they will be examining the biblical material that talks about angels as ministers of justice.

Ask each subgroup to answer the question, "Why is the theme of judgment absent or downplayed in much of the popular literature on angels and in the claims people make about angel encounters when it is so much a part of the biblical record?" Of course, no one answer is correct, and the subgroups will likely come up with a variety of reasons.

Give each group an opportunity to report the highlights of their conversation to the whole group. Identify common threads, but do not try to reach some final conclusion. Keep in mind that the purpose of this activity is to prepare the group for delving into the Bible, not to deride those who do not accept the Bible's authority in this area.

REALITY CHECK
20-30 minutes

Give each subgroup two sheets of newsprint and two markers. The groups should appoint a recorder for each, the first to be headed "Judgment in History," the other, "Judgment of Individuals." As the discussion unfolds, the recorders will jot down the ideas that fit on their sheets.

The subgroups will be looking at a variety of Scripture passages to find principles and examples of angels as ministers of justice. They will examine the passages assigned to them and answer the questions listed below. Their answers will then be reported to the other subgroups.

- In what ways does the Bible show angels working in the course of history to execute God's judgment? (sheet 1)

- In what ways does the Bible show angels working in the lives of individuals to carry out God's judgment? (sheet 2)

Let the subgroups know that you will be examining the role of angels in God's final judgment next session, even though *In the Company of Angels* refers to it in chapter 8. Where it seems relevant to their work, the groups may draw on other passages and explanations included by Andrew Bandstra in this chapter. Divide the following passages among the groups so that each is assigned at least three. If you have a large group, you may assign passages more than once.

Genesis 3:24	Acts 12:23
Genesis 19:12-13, 23-25	1 Corinthians 6:3
Exodus 12:23	1 Corinthians 10:10
2 Kings 19:35	Hebrews 2:5-9
Psalm 8:4-6	Hebrews 11:28
Matthew 26:53	Revelation 12:7-12
Luke 12:8-9	Revelation 16:4-6

When they are done, ask the groups to report their findings to the others, using the two sheets of newsprint.

PERSONAL CONNECTION
10-15 minutes

For this activity, people will continue to work in subgroups. By this time in the course, it's likely that people have acquired some degree of comfort with being vulnerable in the group, and will be able to profit from some supportive self-disclosure. The idea here is to share areas in which God has changed the direction of our lives. This is not intended to be a probing time of confession. Rather,

it is meant to celebrate how God works to direct us day by day as one expression of justice.

Since this is a highly personal activity, the subgroups will not be reporting to the whole group. And of course, people should understand that participation is voluntary. The groups should avoid going around the circle, since individuals may feel put on the spot to talk. Rather, people should be free to share as they are ready and comfortable. Remind people at the beginning that whatever is said in these groups is confidential. The following questions can be used to stimulate the conversation. You may want to write them on your chalkboard or on a sheet of newsprint.

1. What experiences has God used to grab your attention and change your direction?

2. How did you become aware of God's "judgment" in this area of your life?

3. Do you have any sense of angels being involved in the change God prompted in your life?

Before dismissing people, call the whole group back together and look back at the list of questions for which people want answers. Have any of them been covered in this session? For next time, ask people to read chapter 9, "Ministers of Justice (2)." Ask someone to conclude with a prayer asking God bring your lives into harmony with his righteousness as you prepare for the next session.

MINISTERS OF JUSTICE (2)

SESSION GOALS

- to examine the role of angels in revealing and administering God's justice

- to understand the place of angels in the final judgment

- to be confident of God's sovereign and loving plan for human destiny

- to be motivated to live a righteous life in light of God's plan for the future

- to live with confidence and faith in the face of prolific injustice in the world

MATERIALS

- Bibles for all participants (encourage them to bring their own)

- *In the Company of Angels* (participants should bring their own copy)

- Hospitality table supplies

- Newsprint with T. S. Eliot poem

- Examples of "near death" reports of being welcomed by angels or other spiritual beings

- Questions on newsprint or chalkboard for Imaginative Exploration

- Newsprint pad

- Markers

- Masking tape

- Notebook for recording prayer concerns

ARRIVAL ACTIVITY

Write out and post on a sheet of newsprint the final stanza of "The Hollow Men" by T. S. Eliot (printed below for your convenience). You may substitute some other poetry that talks about the end of the world, if you prefer. The poem is not intended to reflect biblical concepts, nor will you be analyzing it. Rather, it is intended to stimulate conversation as people arrive for this session.

> *This is the way the world ends*
> *This is the way the world ends*
> *This is the way the world ends*
> *Not with a bang but a whimper.*

from "The Hollow Men" by T. S. Eliot

As people come in, ask them to read the poem and discuss various other ideas people have about how the world will end, besides the biblical revelation of Christ's return to establish his eternal Kingdom. Some of the possibilities people may mention are nuclear holocaust, global famine, the collision of earth with a giant asteroid, ecological disaster, being swallowed by a black hole. This is the time for people to say, "I read . . . " or "I heard . . . " The idea is not so much to evaluate these as it is to sort through the diversity of concepts and feelings. If people start talking about God's judgment or the coming of the kingdom of God, encourage them to hold those ideas for later in the session.

After the discussion, when everyone has arrived, call the group together and give people the opportunity to mention prayer concerns. Write them in the prayer notebook and review the prayer concerns from the last session. Then lead the group in a time of silent prayer, asking people to pray for the person sitting immediately to their right and to their left.

IMAGINATIVE EXPLORATION
10-15 minutes

To open this discussion, read or tell about one example of someone who has reported being welcomed by angels or other spiritual beings of light in a "near death" experience. These popular stories are often used as evidence to refute the Bible's theme of a final judgment. So it's important to let the group know that such experiences are not confirmed in Scripture, and that a universal welcome to a new life without judgment, regardless of one's faith, is out of harmony with the message of the Bible. The following is one such report:

> Into the garden came a group of spiritual beings. . . . My escorts, who continued to act as my guides, now told me that I had died prematurely and that this wasn't really a graduation party, but a time to show me what I would receive when I returned at the right time. . . .
>
> "When we 'die,'" my guides said, "we experience nothing more than a transition to another state. . . . " I understood that there are many levels of development, and we will always go to that level where we are most comfortable. Most spirits choose to remain on earth for a short time and comfort their loved ones. . . . They remain to help the loved one's spirit heal.
>
> I also was told that our prayers can benefit both spiritual beings as well as persons on the earth. If there is reason to fear for a departed person's spirit, if there is reason to believe their transition may be difficult or unwanted, we can pray for them and enlist spiritual help.
>
> Betty J. Eadie, *Embraced By the Light,* Placerville, CA: Gold Leaf Press, 1992.

Ask people if they have read or heard of similar accounts, then discuss them using the following questions. You may want to write the questions out on a chalkboard or on newsprint.

1. What do these stories have in common?

2. Some have suggested that these experiences may be a physiological phenomenon, perhaps caused by a shortage of oxygen to the brain. Others have suggested it may be a diabolical deception. Do either of these possibilities seem likely?

3. What perspective or philosophy of human destiny and judgment is implied in these reports? What is the appeal of such thinking?

4. What is missing in these accounts that is central to the biblical view of the final judgment?

REALITY CHECK
20-30 minutes

For today's Reality Check, ask people to divide into two groups. They will be investigating the place of angels in God's plan for the ultimate conclusion of history. Angels figure prominently in judgment as described in the book of Revelation, and one group will focus its attention there. The other group will look at the passages in the other parts of Scripture that talk about angels in judgment.

For each of their assigned passages, the groups should list the functions angels perform in the final judgment. Give each some newsprint and markers so they can record the results of their study and report it to the others.

Group One

Deuteronomy 33:2

Psalm 68:15-18

Acts 7:30, 35, 37-38, 51-53

Galatians 3:19

Hebrews 2:2

Group Two

Revelation 2-3 (churches)

Revelation 8:2-11:15 (trumpets)

Revelation 14:6-11 (announcements)

Revelation 15-16 (plagues and bowls of wrath)

When they are done, ask each group to report the results of its study and post its newsprint sheets. Then, as a whole group, discuss the observations that were made. What themes seem to be common to the place of angels in judgment and the conclusion of human history? What conclusions can we draw?

PERSONAL CONNECTION
10-15 minutes

For many people, including some Christians, contemplating God's final judgment generates fear, detachment from daily life, or fascination with the bizarre. Scripture, however, focuses much more on encouraging righteous living, faithful evangelism, confidence in the face of uncertainty, and courage in hardship.

Bring this session to a conclusion by discussing how belief in God's control of history and human destiny builds confidence for living in faith. Use questions like the following to prompt and direct the discussion. Do not try to develop a complete eschatology (theology of last things), but concentrate on the principles and observations the group made in looking at the role of angels in judgment.

1. What evidence of the reality of the kingdom of God can you see in the church (your congregation, your denomination, the larger church worldwide)?

2. What evidence of God's control of history can you see in your community, your nation, the world?

3. In what ways does the surety of God's judgment help you cope with the injustices of life on personal, local, national, and global levels?

4. In what ways can you draw strength from this perspective that is more reliable than popular, non-biblical fantasies about the conclusion of history?

5. What insights did you gain from reading this chapter of *In the Company of Angels* that help give a perspective on your place in human destiny?

Before dismissing people, look back at the list of questions for which people want answers. Can you mark any of them as having been covered in this session? For next week, ask people to read chapter 10, "Some Disputed Issues about Angels." Conclude with a prayer asking God for clarity in thinking about puzzling issues in preparation for the next session.

SOME DISPUTED ISSUES ABOUT ANGELS

SESSION GOALS

- to seek biblical answers to disputed questions about angels

- to develop guidelines for responding biblically to contemporary debates of popular interest about angels

- to give examples of what we may or may not legitimately conclude about the question of "corporate assignments" for angels

MATERIALS

- Bibles for all participants (encourage them to bring their own)

- *In the Company of Angels* (participants should bring their own copy)

- Hospitality table supplies

- List of Scripture passages for Imaginative Exploration

- Photocopies of questions for Reality Check, one for each participant (see page 43)

- Newsprint pad

- Markers

- Masking tape

- Notebook for recording prayer concerns

ARRIVAL ACTIVITY

In this chapter, Bandstra tackles what he calls "some *really big* disputed issues" about angels. He warns us that the themes dealt with in the chapter are areas where Scripture evidence is scarce and open to debatable interpretations. As people come into the room, ask them to come up with questions they have after reading this chapter. Are there any topics that seemed especially intriguing or ideas which they would like to discuss further? As people formulate questions, write them on a sheet of newsprint. As you fill each sheet, post it where you can refer to it later in the session.

After people have had a chance to come up with questions, ask them to form subgroups of four or five. Request

prayer concerns, then write them in the prayer notebook and review the prayer concerns from the last session. Ask people to pray for each other in their groups.

IMAGINATIVE EXPLORATION

10-15 minutes

Direct the attention of the subgroups to the questions brainstormed during the Arrival Activity and refer them to the issues Bandstra covers in chapter 10: Are there national angels? Church angels? Are the twenty-four elders a special class of angels? What about the "principalities and powers"? Remind the group that often we have questions about which the Bible just doesn't say much, if anything. Sometimes these may be matters of mere curiosity—What do angels look like? Other times they may be issues that don't have direct bearing on our faith—Can angels be detected by modern scientific equipment? And still other times our human questions may actually lead us away from faith in Christ—How can I initiate communication with angels?

Remind the subgroups of John Calvin's principle that we are not to fall into speculation or superstition but to seek what is true and sure, profitable, and beneficial (session 2, chapter 1 of *In the Company of Angels*). Using that as a model, the subgroups are to formulate other guidelines that are based on or are consistent with Scripture for handling questions about which there is dispute and uncertainty.

Each group should try to come up with three guidelines and write them on a sheet of newsprint. To help formulate these guidelines, they may look up the following Scripture passages, which you have written on a chalkboard or sheet of newsprint.

- Psalm 131

- John 20:31

- 2 Corinthians 12:2-6

- 1 Timothy 6:3-5

- Titus 3:8-9

When the groups have come up with three guidelines, go from one group to the next, each reporting one of its guidelines. After all the guidelines have been reported, each subgroup should post its written list. These will help direct the discussion in the next activity.

REALITY CHECK
20-30 minutes

In popular thinking, the concept of guardian angels has been extended beyond individuals to include collective entities such as territories, nations, ethnic groups, or churches. Along with that a corresponding concept of demonic forces with similar corporate assignments has come into being. Such thinking has been put to highly imaginative use in fiction such as Frank Peretti's novels *This Present Darkness* and *Piercing the Darkness*. Unfortunately, writers often leave the impression that the forces of evil are more powerful than the forces of good.

Nevertheless, as Andrew Bandstra points out (pp. 93-96), some passages of the Bible do seem to suggest at least the possibility of angels being assigned to territories, nations, ethnic groups, or churches. The group will examine these passages as a way of using the guidelines they developed for dealing with disputed issues and as a case study in how we might handle other disputed issues.

Working together as one large group, ask people to look up the relevant passages (printed below). For each passage, they should keep in mind the list of guidelines they wrote in the previous step.

- Deuteronomy 32:8

- Daniel 10:13, 20

- Ephesians 6:12

- Colossians 2:10, 15

- Hebrews 2:5-9

- Revelation 1:20-2:1 (note also 2:8, 12, 18; 3:1, 7, 14)

As a group, discuss each of the passages, using some or all of the following questions as a guide. It may be helpful for you to photocopy the passages and the questions (printed below) for each member of your group. For easy photocopying, the passages and the questions are also printed on page 43.

1. Which of the guidelines for dealing with disputed issues seem most relevant to the question of "corporate assignments" for angels?

2. What can we confidently conclude about "corporate assignments" for angels from these Scripture passages? What ideas about "corporate assignments" for angels are clearly excluded by these passages?

3. How might the assignment of angels to churches be different from their assignment to territories, nations, or ethnic groups? In what ways might they be similar? What biblical evidence supports these suggestions?

4. Are these Scripture passages examples of specific cases for particular purposes or are they examples of a general pattern that extends to all locations and all ages, even our generation? How would you decide?

PERSONAL CONNECTION
10-15 minutes

This session has been long on questions but short on answers. Ask the people in your group if they feel satisfied with the way their questions were handled. Give them a chance to come back to any of their questions about this chapter in particular that they would still like to comment on. Although the issues addressed in the chapter will likely never be "solved" in the sense of feeling total certainty about what the Bible teaches about "corporate assignments" for angels, Bandstra's careful treatment of the relevant passages and your group's formulation of guidelines for evaluating disputed issues will equip us to deal with these and other thorny questions about angels.

To conclude the session, ask people to think about and discuss Bandstra's question about the "benefit" we might receive as Christians from believing in the "corporate assignments" of angels. Does it make any difference to our faith, one way or another? You may want to sum up the discussion with Bandstra's statement that "there is a very close tie between heaven and earth: what happens on earth has a profound effect in heaven, and what happens in heaven has a profound effect upon earth."

Before dismissing people, look back at the list of questions for which people want answers. Have any of them been covered in this session? For next time, ask people to read chapter 11, "Do Angels Really Exist?" This is also a good time to review Hebrews 1 and 2 as well. Encourage people to poll their friends, relatives, and neighbors before the next session to find out whether or not they believe in the existence of angels.

Ask someone to conclude with a prayer asking God to equip people for ministry when disputes arise and to strengthen the church in this generation.

"REALITY CHECK" PASSAGES AND QUESTIONS

Passages

Deuteronomy 32:8

Daniel 10:13, 20

Ephesians 6:12

Colossians 2:10, 15

Hebrews 2:5-9

Revelation 1:20-2:1 (note also 2:8, 12, 18; 3:1, 7, 14)

Questions for Discussion

1. Which of the guidelines for dealing with disputed issues seem most relevant to the question of "corporate assignments" for angels?

2. What can we confidently conclude about "corporate assignments" for angels from these Scripture passages? What ideas about "corporate assignments" for angels are clearly excluded by these passages?

3. How might the assignment of angels to churches be different from their assignment to territories, nations, or ethnic groups? In what ways might they be similar? What biblical evidence supports these suggestions?

4. Are these Scripture passages examples of specific cases for particular purposes or are they examples of a general pattern that extends to all locations and all ages, even our generation? How would you decide?

DO ANGELS REALLY EXIST?

SESSION GOALS

- to evaluate various ideas about the existence of angels

- to compare the perspectives of "Christian" scholars with biblical teaching about the existence of angels

- to understand the biblical teaching about the existence of angels

MATERIALS LIST

- Bibles for all participants (encourage them to bring their own)

- *In the Company of Angels* (participants should bring their own copy)

- Hospitality table supplies

- Newsprint pad

- Markers

- Masking tape

- Notebook for recording prayer concerns

ARRIVAL ACTIVITY

Last week, you encouraged people to make an informal survey among their family, friends, and acquaintances on the question of whether or not angels really exist. As they come in, ask people to report the results of their findings on your chalkboard or on a sheet of newsprint, which you will have prepared ahead of time. Prepare the sheet by making two columns, one headed "Unchurched" and the other "Active in a Christian church." Ask people to record in the appropriate column the percentage of people they asked who believe angels really exist. If some people did not make a survey, ask them to record their best guess at the moment.

You may wish to calculate the average percentages and write them down as well. Until you are ready to start the session, people may informally discuss any insights or observations that arise from this informal poll. You may be surprised to discover that many unchurched people say they believe in the existence of angels, and that active church people may say they do not believe in the existence of angels. For example, authentic Christian believers who are concerned about biblical integrity may shy away from expressing too much confidence in the existence of angels as a reaction to the fanciful and misleading stereotypes that are affirmed in popular literature.

When everyone has arrived and you have looked at the results of your survey, call the group together. Give people a chance to mention prayer concerns and write them in the prayer notebook. Review the prayer concerns from the last session. Ask the group to form five subgroups, then take a few minutes to pray for each other.

IMAGINATIVE EXPLORATION
10-15 minutes

In the Company of Angels quotes Abraham Kuyper as saying, "Either we honor the world of angels as God has revealed that world in Scripture, or run the danger of falling back into a naturalistic religion, holding only to those things that we can see." In response, Andrew Bandstra writes, "I think Kuyper is right. What do you think?"

In order to answer Bandstra's question, the five subgroups formed during the opening prayer will be looking at one of the five "Christian" perspectives about the existence of angels Bandstra covers in the chapter. Each of these perspectives attempts to explain angels in a way that is consistent with a scientific worldview.

- no angels (pp. 114-115)

- near denial (p. 115)

- not a specifically Christian teaching (pp. 116-117)

- myth (pp. 117-119)

- angels as temporary messengers (pp. 119-120)

Assign one of the perspectives covered in the chapter to each of the subgroups. The groups' task is to understand the position and be able to explain it to the others in the class. Using the information from the chapter as well as their own ideas, they should make a case for their assigned position. Allow time for each subgroup to make their report to the others.

REALITY CHECK
20-30 minutes

Hebrews 1 and 2 draws together more information about angels than any other part of the Bible, though it is teaching directly about Christ and only indirectly about angels. Your group examined this passage in some detail at the beginning of the course. Today you will return to it again for what it can teach about the reality of angels.

For this activity, the subgroups will return to the scholarly perspectives they were analyzing earlier. This time they will be using the Hebrews 1 and 2 passage to compare and contrast their assigned perspective with the biblical information about angels.

They should answer the following questions based on the information in Hebrews 1 and 2, recording their insights on sheets of newsprint headed with one of the questions printed below.

1. In what ways is this perspective similar to biblical input on the reality of angels?

2. In what ways is this perspective different from biblical input on the reality of angels?

After the groups have recorded their answers to the questions, allow time for all the groups to report their conclusions. Based on their answers to these questions and to the work done in the Imaginative Exploration section, ask everyone to discuss Andrew Bandstra's question, "What do you think?"

PERSONAL CONNECTION
10-15 minutes

Assemble as one whole group for the final discussion of this session. Let people know that this discussion will prepare them for the final session of the course. Encourage them to draw on insights they gained as they worked in their subgroups and as they listened to the other subgroups report. The questions printed below can be used to help focus the discussion. You may want to take some notes so that you can target the final session to the specific interests and concerns of people in your group.

1. What difference does it make for us to believe in the reality of angels? How does it affect our faith? How does it affect daily life as a Christian?

2. What do we lose if we don't believe in the existence of angels?

3. What do we gain by believing in the existence of angels?

Before dismissing people, look back at the list of questions for which people want answers. Can you mark any of them as having been covered in this session? For next time, ask people to read chapter 12, "The Benefit of Believing in Angels." Then ask someone to conclude with a prayer asking God for spiritual discernment as people explore the practical benefits of believing in angels.

THE BENEFIT OF BELIEVING IN ANGELS

SESSION GOALS

- to recognize that angels serve for our benefit

- to identify how believing in angels benefits Christians

- to draw on these benefits for ourselves and our church

- to enrich and strengthen our thinking about God's work in our lives and our world

MATERIALS

- Bibles for all participants (encourage them to bring their own)

- *In the Company of Angels* (participants should bring their own copy)

- Hospitality table supplies

- Photocopies of Reality Check questions, one for each participant (see page 48)

- Notebook for recording prayer concerns

- 3" x 5" card for each group participant

ARRIVAL ACTIVITY

By this time, you and your group are probably very aware of how much attention angels are receiving both within and outside of the church. As people arrive ask them to talk informally about what they have learned about angels during this course. Were there any surprises?

When you are ready to begin, call the group together. Ask if people have prayer concerns and write them in the prayer notebook. (You may want to plan some sort of "reunion" for this group in which you would socialize and pray. If so, the prayer notebook could be valuable for such an occasion.) Review the prayer concerns from the last session. In a single circle, invite people to pray for others in the group to be aware of God's reality and involvement in their lives.

IMAGINATIVE EXPLORATION
15 minutes

This role-play exercise will help people draw together what they have learned during this course and sharpen their ability to communicate a biblical perspective to people who do not accept the Bible's unique authority. Ask people to form pairs. Each person will take turns playing the roles of presenter and listener.

The person whose birthday is next will be the first presenter. This person's task is to explain a biblical view of angels to his or her partner. The listener will act the part of a non-Christian who does not believe in the existence of angels. Before starting the conversations, allow a few minutes for each person to prepare mentally the approach they want to take as both the presenter and as the listener.

After the first presenters have had a few minutes to talk, switch roles. When both partners have had the opportunity to role-play the roles of presenter and listener, allow a little time for the pairs to talk about their experience by answering the following questions.

- Does the popularity of angels give unique opportunities for presenting the gospel? How can we make the most of these opportunities?

REALITY CHECK
20-30 minutes

Andrew Bandstra suggests several benefits of believing in angels: to comfort us in our weakness and protect us, to focus our thinking on and about God, and to encourage telling the stories of Christ's grace in the family of God. These benefits are enjoyed by believers whether or not they ever have a personal encounter with angels. Have your group explore how these benefits work in the account of the angels protecting Elisha and his servant in 2 Kings 6:8-23. Instead of simply having people look up and read the passage individually, your group may want to take parts and read the piece as a reader's theater. Ask for volunteers to take the parts of the narrator, the king of Aram, Elisha, an officer, and Elisha's servant.

You may wish to photocopy the following questions to use in examining the role of angels in this story (for your convenience, they're printed separately on page 48):

1. If you stopped reading the story at verse 17 and did not know how it comes out, what would you expect to happen next?

2. Why do you think God used blindness rather than direct angelic battle to deliver Elisha? What function do the angels that surround the Aramean army have?

3. How aware of the angels do you think Elisha was before he asked God to let his servant see them? What can you conclude about the connection of our awareness of angels and our receiving the benefits of believing in them?

4. What benefits do Elisha, his servant, the King of Israel, and the people of Israel receive from God in this incident? What part do the angels play in their receiving these benefits?

5. How would the Arameans have described the angels in this incident? Consider their reactions to being struck blind, to being led into Samaria, and being released by the Israelites? What does this tell us about how unbelievers understand angels?

When your group has had some time to probe this incident, ask them to connect their conversation with this session's chapter of *In the Company of Angels* by discussing the following questions.

1. Which of the benefits of believing in angels described by Andrew Bandstra can you identify in this episode?

2. Can you identify any other benefits in this episode of believing in angels?

3. Can you think of other benefits of believing in angels from what we have investigated in this course?

PERSONAL CONNECTION
10-15 minutes

Distribute 3" x 5" cards to each member of the group; then ask people to write an answer to the following question on their cards. "How can I benefit most from what God wants to give through angels?"

If the group is very large (twenty or more), divide into subgroups of four to six people. Invite each person to read aloud to the others what he or she has written on the card. After everyone has shared their answers, collect the cards. These will give you a way of measuring your effectiveness in leading the group. You may also wish to duplicate what people have written on their cards and distribute the results to the whole group, perhaps sending them along with a note written as a follow-up to the course after about a month.

Before dismissing people for the last time, look back at the list of questions for which people want answers. Can you mark any of them as having been covered in this session? If any have not been handled, you will want to address them, at least briefly. Of course, you may not be able to provide answers for some of the things people want to know. If that's the case don't be embarrassed to say so.

Conclude with a prayer thanking God for each member of the group and for what you have learned together during this course.

We invite you to let us know about your experience in leading this course. Did people find it meaningful? What would the group suggest doing differently? Send your reactions, suggestions for improvement, questions, and comments to

CRC Publications
2850 Kalamazoo Ave. SE
Grand Rapids, MI 49560

REALITY CHECK QUESTIONS FOR DISCUSSION

Read 2 Kings 6:8-23

1. If you stopped reading the story at verse 17 and did not know how it comes out, what would you expect to happen next?

2. Why do you think God used blindness rather than direct angelic battle to deliver Elisha? What function do the angels that surround the Aramean army have?

3. How aware of the angels do you think Elisha was before he asked God to let his servant see them? What can you conclude about the connection of our awareness of angels and our receiving the benefits of believing in them?

4. What benefits do Elisha, his servant, the King of Israel, and the people of Israel receive from God in this incident? What part do the angels play in their receiving these benefits?

5. How would the Arameans have described the angels in this incident? Consider their reactions to being struck blind, to being led into Samaria, and being released by the Israelites? What does this tell us about how unbelievers understand angels?

After discussing the above, connect your conversation with chapter 12 of *In the Company of Angels* by using the following questions:

1. Which of the benefits of believing in angels described by Andrew Bandstra can you identify in this episode?

2. Can you identify any other benefits in this episode of believing in angels?

3. Can you think of other benefits of believing in angels from what we have investigated in this course?